10649252

EVERYDAY EVANGELISM

MATT QUEEN

SEMINARY HILL PRESS

Seminary Hill Press
2001 West Seminary Drive
Fort Worth, Texas 76115

Everyday Evangelism
By Matt Queen
Copyright © 2015 by Matt Queen
ISBN: 978-0-9839392-4-5
Publication Date: April 2015

CONTENTS

Introduction

In 1950, the Southern Baptist Convention was comprised of 7,079,889 members. The 27,788 churches to which these members belonged reported 376,085 baptisms, meaning that one person was baptized for every 19 members. In 2011, the convention's 45,764 churches reported 15,978,112 members and 333,341 baptisms. The baptism-to-member ratio increased to one baptism for every 48 members—8,898,223 more members and 17,976 more churches resulted in fewer baptisms and a higher baptism-to-member ratio!

While certain factors, such as the increasing number of churches that fail to report their Annual Church Profile, explain some of the discrepancy, this higher baptism-to-member ratio identifies a glaring deficiency among Southern Baptist churches. The need of the hour in our churches is that we practice *everyday evangelism*. Everyday evangelism is an atmosphere in which church members regularly share their faith as a natural part of their daily lives.

Motivating and mobilizing your church in *everyday evangelism* can be a daunting endeavor. Nevertheless, you have decided to read this book because you are up to the task! A simple strategy to assist you as you create a culture of *everyday evangelism* in your church includes the following:

1. PRAY

Seek the Lord's direction, power, and blessing for this evangelistic endeavor through prayer. Regardless of how well-intentioned and prepared the personal evangelist is, he needs the Lord's direction and wisdom in order to begin this endeavor and see it sustained in his church. Ask God to empower you in making evangelism contagious in your church. Involve your church members in regular times of focused prayer for the salvation of the lost in your community. Also, pray that the Lord will begin to stir a passion for consistent evangelism within other church members' hearts. Lastly, seek the blessing of God upon this endeavor. Apart from His blessing, any attempt to promote an *everyday evangelism* kind of atmosphere in your church will fail.

2. COMMIT

Make a personal commitment before God to practice intentional, *everyday evangelism*. Ask God to help you keep this commitment. Share this commitment with others in your church, and ask them to encourage and keep you accountable to fulfill it. Consider your daily agenda, and intentionally schedule evangelism into your day.

3. ENCOURAGE

Invite others in your church to commit to daily, intentional evangelism. Not everyone you invite to become a consistent personal evangelist will make this commitment, but some fellow church members will commit if someone will only ask them. Periodically send those who make such commitments notes, emails, or text messages to encourage them and assure them you are praying for them as they evangelize.

4. EVANGELIZE

Ask those who make commitments to accompany you during the church's scheduled evangelism outings. Keep in mind that some of those who commit are would-be evangelists, needing someone to teach them how to share the gospel. Share some basic gospel presentations with them (*e.g.*, The Roman's Road, Steps to Peace with God, One Verse Evangelism) and encourage them to memorize at least one presentation. Demonstrate how to utilize the gospel presentation they select in live evangelism encounters. Also, invite them to begin to participate in the evangelistic conversations, assuring them that they can do so at their own pace and that you will assist them in the conversation if they experience any trouble.

Others who commit to evangelize have confidence in sharing the gospel but have never equipped someone else to evangelize. Encourage them to identify two fellow church members to train in evangelism. Make yourself available to advise and counsel them whenever they have questions about best training practices. Over time, also challenge them to teach those they have trained in evangelism how they, too, can equip and train future would-be evangelists.

Thank you for your interest in *Everyday Evangelism*. This book aims to encourage the pastors, staff, deacons, and members of local churches everywhere to practice *everyday evangelism*. In it, readers will find essays that present biblically driven evangelism themes that seek to motivate readers and their churches in a commitment to practice *everyday evangelism*. Readers, beware, this book will challenge some of today's most commonly accepted evangelism misnomers by first identifying how evangelism was practiced in Scripture and then applying biblical principles to inform contemporary practices of evangelism.

May the Lord bless your evangelistic efforts and once again breathe revival into believers and churches across our nation.

Matt Queen
Associate Professor of Evangelism
L.R. Scarborough Chair of Evangelism ("The Chair of Fire")
Associate Dean for Doctoral Programs
Southwestern Baptist Theological Seminary
Fort Worth, Texas

CHAPTER 1

Toward an Understanding of Evangelism

Three telephone pole installation crews sought to win an installation contract with the local telephone company. The phone company decided that it would put all three crews to a test. Each team would be given one day to set as many telephone poles in the ground as possible.

When the day was over, the first crew reported to the phone company official that they had installed 35 poles in the ground. The company representative was very impressed! The second crew reported that they mounted 32 poles in the ground. The phone official relayed to the second crew, "That's good, but it's not good enough." Finally, he asked the third crew: "How many poles did you set in the ground?" The foreman proudly announced, "Two!" "Two?" asked the phone company official. "Why are you so proud of installing two telephone poles? This team set 32 poles, and the other team set 35." "Well, yeah," said the foreman, "but look at how much they left sticking out of the ground."

WHAT EVANGELISM IS NOT[1]

In the same way that the third crew misunderstood the task at hand, many would-be personal evangelists want to practice *everyday evangelism*, but they misunderstand what evangelism is. In order to understand the

---

1 C. E. Autrey popularized the following approach of articulating misconceptions about evangelism in order to define evangelism biblically in *Basic Evangelism* (Grand Rapids: Zondervan, 1959), 26-30. Alvin Reid also utilized this approach in articulating misconceptions of evangelism in order to define evangelism in *Evangelism Handbook: Biblical, Spiritual, Intentional, Missional* (Nashville: B&H, 2009), 17-22.

meaning of evangelism, churches and believers first must understand
what evangelism is not. Consider the following common misconceptions
of evangelism:

1. Use Words When Necessary[2]

Some churches and believers think they practice evangelism on the
basis of their moral and upright lifestyles, apart from actually verbalizing
the gospel. They believe the difference that Christ has made in their lives
on its own, without a verbal declaration of the gospel, will raise unbelievers' curiosities and lead them to approach believers with their inquiries
and interests in the gospel. Practitioners of this approach fondly assert a
common misnomer attributed to Francis of Assisi: "Preach the gospel;
use words when necessary."[3]

Tommy Kiker, a Southwestern Baptist Theological Seminary pastoral ministries professor, retorts, "'Go, preach the gospel, use words when
necessary,' is like saying, 'Go, feed the hungry, use food when necessary.'" Believers should live moral and upright lives, but they have been
called to live according to the highest standard of righteousness, that
is, holiness (cf., Eph 1:4; 5:27; 1 Pet 1:15-16). While believers' lifestyles
must match the demands of the gospel, believers must not forget that
evangelism necessitates a verbal proclamation of the gospel. They, like
first-century believers, are called to preach the gospel (cf., Acts 10:42;
Rom 10:15; 1 Cor 1:17; Gal 1:15-16; Eph 3:8; and 2 Tim 4:1-2), not
merely to live holy lives.

On this point, consider the model of the apostles and first-century
believers. They do not "use words when necessary" when they practice
evangelism in the New Testament. Words are necessary for personal
evangelists in the New Testament! Examples of New Testament evangelism occur in the context of proclamation, not mere demonstration or
duty alone. In fact, the New Testament addresses this kind of approach

---

2   Reid coins this "The Mute Approach" in Ibid., 17-18.
3   Mark Galli discredits this quote being attributed to Francis in *Francis of Assisi and His
     World* (Downers Grove: InterVarsity, 2003). Also, he states the following in a subse-
     quent Christianity Today article: This saying is carted out whenever someone wants
     to suggest that Christians talk about the gospel too much and live the gospel too little.
     Fair enough—that can be a problem. Much of the rhetorical power of the quotation
     comes from the assumption that Francis not only said it but lived it. The problem
     is that he did not say it. Nor did he live it." "Speak the Gospel, Use Deeds When
     Necessary;" accessed on May 8, 2014, http://www. christianitytoday.com/ct/2009/may-
     web-only/120-42.0.html.

only once, and it refers to a marriage in which a believing wife is married to an unbelieving husband (1 Pet 3:1-2). As such, this passage's specific context and intent is not prescriptive for all believers, that is, for men and women to which this situation does not apply; nor should it be adopted by all believers as a normative evangelistic approach.

2. Professionals Only[4]

This misconception of evangelism advances a narrative that only certain people can, or should, evangelize. A number of churches and believers consider evangelism to be a task for pastors, preachers, and evangelists. They are convinced that only those with "the gift of evangelism" have the ability and the responsibility to evangelize.

This mindset fails for many reasons. First, the Bible never describes "the gift of evangelism." Paul does identify "the gift of the evangelist" (Eph 4:11), but he explains that these spiritually-gifted evangelists equip the saints for ministry (Eph 4:12-13). Second, the evangelistic enterprise of the church cannot advance through the evangelism practiced by evangelists alone because God has ordained that all believers evangelize. Nowhere in the Gospels does our Lord appoint only spiritually-gifted evangelists to fulfill the Great Commission on their own. If He had, not all of those first disciples who received the Great Commission would have evangelized others or encouraged the disciples they made to evangelize, but they did! Last, if the task of world evangelization falls only upon spiritually gifted evangelists, then Jesus' promise to be with us always (Matt 28:20) applies only to evangelists.

3. Anything and Everything[5]

Several think that evangelism occurs at any and every activity occurring in their churches. While churches and believers should do everything they do with an eye toward evangelism, the sad reality is that they do not. Because churches and believers do lots of different kinds of things, they convince themselves that their activities constitute evangelism, even if they haven't shared the gospel in the course of all they

---

4   Reid calls this approach "The Professionals Need Only Apply Approach" in *Evangelism Handbook*, 18-20.

5   Autrey articulates this approach in *Basic Evangelism*, 26-27, and Alvin Reid calls this concept "The Cop Out Approach" in *Evangelism Handbook*, 20-22.

are doing. Thus, they believe when they have a pot luck meal and many unbelievers attend, they have evangelized. Some have convinced themselves that because many guests visit their church on a particular Sunday morning, evangelism has occurred. Still yet, others think they have evangelized on the basis that they have offered a ministry (*e.g.*, Vacation Bible School, a financial workshop, a marriage enrichment weekend, a food pantry, or a clothes closet) to the community. While all of these endeavors and situations are commendable and can be outlets to evangelize, those who think anything and everything they do is evangelism must realize that if the gospel of Jesus Christ is not verbally proclaimed and offered to those in attendance, then an event, not evangelism, has taken place.

4. When I Get Time

Some tell themselves they will evangelize when they feel like it or have the time to do so. This mindset inevitably relegates evangelism to a pastime activity, if it occurs at all. In order for *everyday evangelism* to take place, it must be intentional and sometimes even planned. Those who fail to plan time to evangelize will fail to find time to evangelize.

5. We are All Okay[6]

Either telling others they are already God's children, or simply believing it to be true, constitutes a "we are all okay" misconception about evangelism. One specific example of this approach can be found in Steve Smith and Ying Kai's book, *T4T: A Discipleship Re-Revolution*. In it, Smith says that Kai began evangelistic conversations by stating, "Congratulations, you are God's child! The problem is that you are lost, but I will show you how to be saved."[7] The Bible teaches that all people are God's creation (*cf.* Gen 1:27), but only repentance of sin and faith in Jesus Christ alone appropriates men and women as the children of God (*cf.* John 1:12; Rom 8:16; 9:7-9; and 1 John 3:1). If we tell our hearers that they are God's children already, then why would they want to repent and believe? In fact, taking this statement to its logical conclusions can promote a type of "Christian" universalism that assumes everyone will be

---

6   Autrey refers to this approach as "syncretism" in *Basic Evangelism*, 29-30.
7   Steve Smith with Ying Kai, *T4T: A Discipleship Re-Revolution* (Monument: WIGTake Resources, 2011), 217.

saved in the end. *Everyday evangelists* aren't spiritual gurus; they are God's mouthpieces that sound forth God's love for the world through Jesus Christ's death, burial, and resurrection and call for everyone, everywhere to repent of their sins and believe in Jesus Christ alone for salvation.

6. Shaming Others

Personal evangelists, who on their own authority and/or for their own pleasure condemn and shame others during an evangelistic encounter exemplify the "shaming others" mentality. In this approach, evangelists seek to make listeners feel bad about themselves apart from the conviction of the Holy Spirit. Extreme cases of this attitude include so-called evangelists berating others without either talking to them or sharing the gospel with them.

Everyday evangelists must convey to their listeners that all sinners are judged because they have not believed in Jesus Christ (John 3:18-19, 36); but they must not neglect to tell those who hear that Jesus Christ died on the cross for their sins, and if they will repent of their sins and believe in Jesus Christ, they can be forgiven and declared righteous in Jesus Christ. Likewise, sinners must be told that hell awaits them if they do not believe and repent, but everyday evangelists must tell them in such a way that their listeners realize that the evangelists care for their souls and want them to avoid hell through Jesus Christ and Him alone.

7. Winning at All Costs

Some believers seem more interested in winning arguments than they do winning souls. In their well-meaning attempts to explain and defend the gospel, they end up arguing their point in hopes that their listeners will concede that the evangelist is correct and they are wrong. The apostle Paul states five times in 1 Corinthians 9:19-23 that he has done everything he can do under the law of Christ to win others, but by "win" he neither means simply to convince them nor to triumph over them. Rather, he intends "win" to mean leading them to faith in Christ (1 Cor 9:22b). Therefore, everyday evangelists should share the gospel with complete confidence in its veracity but do so for the reason Christ evangelized—so that people will repent and believe the gospel (Mark 1:15).

8. Sheep Stealing

Other well-meaning church members encourage a member from another church to unite with their church and call what they do evangelism, when in reality they exercise "sheep stealing." This practice proves unhealthy and essentially becomes a kind of spiritual cannibalism. Although every church should encourage an inviting and accepting atmosphere for believers that are searching for a church to which they can belong, this characteristic on its own merits does not constitute evangelism.

Churches and believers do not evangelize believers, they evangelize unbelievers. Furthermore, evangelism is not inviting already established believers to become members of a church (though such an invitation is encouraged if evangelists find believers who are not actively involved in a Bible-believing church). Rather, evangelism is inviting unbelievers to respond to the good news of Jesus Christ through repentance and faith by becoming disciples of Jesus Christ, professing their newfound faith through believer's baptism, and being taught obedience to all the commands of Christ (primarily in the local church in which they will be baptized and to which they will belong).

9. Visit My Church[8]

Similar to "sheep stealing," some simply invite unbelievers to attend their churches. While church members should invite unbelievers to their churches, any invitation to attend church that does not also invite unbelievers to receive Christ cannot be considered evangelism. What about unbelievers who never accept the invitation to attend church in order to hear the gospel? Or, what about those unbelievers who intend to come to church but suddenly die before Sunday comes? What if some unbelievers do attend church, but the pastor does not preach the gospel to them? In order to evangelize unbelievers, *everyday evangelists* must present enough of the gospel to them that they know what Jesus did for them on the cross and from the tomb, as well as invite them to receive Jesus as their Savior and Lord.

---

8   Autrey utilizes this approach in *Basic Evangelism*, 27-28.

10. Another Notch in My Belt[9]

"Belt-notching" is a popular idiom that refers to those who boast of some success or achievement for the purpose of bringing attention to themselves. Believers who only concern themselves with adding another notch in their belts act out of pride in order to receive recognition for those who, upon hearing the gospel, profess faith in Jesus Christ. Scripture exhorts evangelists not to boast or seek credit for what God does in the gospel through their evangelism (1 Cor 1:31; 9:16; 2 Cor 10:12-18; Gal 5:25-26; 6:13-15).

11. Manipulation

Unfortunately, some who practice evangelism attempt to manipulate and pressure their hearers into making professions of faith. Those who use manipulation neglect the convicting work of the Holy Spirit and attempt to force their hearers into a decision for which the Spirit of God has not prepared their hearts. Those who practice such things would do well to keep in mind that if they can talk people into making a decision, then others can talk them into making a completely opposite decision. Worse yet, manipulators can foster a false assurance of salvation within those who have not actually repented and believed in Christ, if not altogether harden sinners' hearts to receive the gospel because they believe they are saved when in reality they are not.

WHAT EVANGELISM IS

With so many misconceptions abounding, what then is evangelism? Any church or believer desiring to practice consistent *everyday evangelism* must understand the meaning of evangelism. Evangelism is *that Spirit-empowered activity in which disciples of Jesus Christ give an intentional, verbal, and complete witness to the life, death, burial, and resurrection of Jesus Christ, calling unbelievers to become disciples of Jesus Christ by repenting of their sins and placing their faith in Jesus Christ alone.* Evangelism aims that those who hear the gospel and become disciples of Jesus Christ will then become members of a local church through believer's baptism in the name of the Father, Son, and Spirit and will be taught obedience to all the commands

---

9   Reid explains this approach by combining "The Sheep Stealing Approach" and "The Belt-Notching Approach" under what he calls "The Numbers Game Approach" in *Evangelism Handbook*, 18. However, "The Sheep Stealing Approach" appears to be a different concept than "The Belt-Notching Approach."

of Jesus Christ.

WHAT IS A SIMPLE EVANGELISTIC APPROACH?

Having identified the most common misnomers concerning evangelism, as well as defining evangelism and its aim, does a simple evangelistic approach exist that can assist believers in practicing *everyday evangelism*? Intentionality in evangelism isn't simply knowing that believers should evangelize; rather it is making a plan to evangelize consistently and then executing it. Any strategy that encourages believers to evangelize will result in *everyday evangelism*. One simple approach everyday evangelists can utilize as they intentionally seek to evangelize unbelievers includes the following:

1. Pray

Everyday evangelists who do not pray will find their evangelism meeting with failure. During their quiet times, periodically throughout every day, and before they gather for planned times of evangelism, believers should pray for God's Spirit to precede their witness and to empower their witness for Jesus with boldness. In addition, everyday evangelists should keep a list of unbelievers' names for whose salvation they will consistently intercede before God. Praying for these requests will not guarantee that everyone that hears the gospel will respond in faith, nor does it mean that everyday evangelists will not experience spiritual attacks. However, failure to pray in preparation for evangelism essentially forfeits the blessings of God and leads to spiritual vulnerability.

2. Identify and Utilize Points of Contact

Personal evangelists will find no shortage of people who need to hear the gospel; however, those finding trouble identifying those with whom they'll share the gospel will want to utilize points of contact. They can find points of contact beginning with those with whom they have relationships (*e.g.*, unbelieving family, friends, and neighbors). In addition, they can approach people like their barber/hair stylist, their dentist, or solicitors who visit their homes.

Some who desire to evangelize have decided to do so if God will provide them with opportunities to do so. However, by "opportunities" they mean someone coming up to them and asking them what they must do to be saved. Rarely, if ever, will these hopeful evangelists get these "opportunities." Therefore, consider evangelistic opportunities from God as those people with whom evangelists come into contact that their spiritual state is unknown or that it is known that they need Christ.

3. Articulate a Transition Statement

Once evangelists have identified points of contact for evangelism, they need to engage these people in conversation. Because God is the creator of all things, evangelists should anticipate and listen for topics that arise in the conversation to transition to the gospel. Some examples of these transitions include: 1) discussions concerning an earthly father can lead to discussions about the Heavenly Father's love as demonstrated by sending Jesus Christ to die for everyone's sins; 2) information about important life events can lead to personal evangelistic testimonies about how they came to Christ; 3) concerns about impending death or the uncertainty of life can lead to conversations about how believing in the gospel provides the only way for people to go heaven; and 4) details about others' weekend activities can lead to dialogues about believers' Sunday church services and ultimately to the gospel.

4. Present the Gospel

Utilize any presentation of the gospel that is both biblically accurate and easy to remember. However, evangelists desiring to share the gospel in a more natural, extemporaneous way will want to ensure they present the core elements of the gospel. First, they must convey the reality and consequences of sin in the lives of their hearers. Second, they must declare the life, death, burial, and resurrection of Jesus Christ and how He alone serves as the provision for everyone to be reconciled to God. Last, they must explain to their listeners that reconciliation with God through Jesus can only occur if they will repent of their sins and believe in Jesus Christ alone for salvation.

5. Encourage Questions for Clarification

After an evangelist gives a complete presentation of the gospel, he should ask his hearers the following questions: 1) "Do you understand what I have shared with you?" 2) "Do you have any questions about what I have shared with you?" and 3) "Have you ever made this kind of decision?"

If the person responds, "Yes," then ask him to share with you when he made this decision and to provide some of the details of how he received Christ. If he testifies of having experienced biblical conversion, then encourage him to become an everyday evangelist if he is not consistently evangelizing.

6. Invite Your Hearers to Receive Christ

If the person with whom you are sharing the gospel does not articulate a biblical conversion experience, then explain to him how his experience falls short according to Scripture, and invite him to receive Jesus through repentance and faith. However, if he responds, "No," then ask him if he will repent of his sins and believe in Jesus' death for his sins and resurrection from the dead for his salvation.

Many of those who hear the gospel will decline to repent and believe. With complete sincerity, devoid of any manipulation, an everyday evangelist should advise someone who declines of the eternal consequences of his decision and encourage him to reconsider it. If he still rejects the offer of the gospel, then leave him with a gospel tract that includes your contact information[10] or the contact information of your local church.

On the other hand, if the other person indicates that he would like to repent and believe, then summarize the gospel and emphasize the demands of the gospel. Ask him if he understands the decision he is about to make. Depending on his response, do the following:

1. If he indicates, under the conviction of the Holy Spirit, that he wants to repent and believe, then instruct him to call on the Lord for salvation (Rom 10:13) in repentance and faith. Remind him that Jesus, not his prayer, will save him and that he receives his salvation by calling on the name of the Lord in repentance and faith. Encourage him to express 1) his sinfulness before God, 2) his need for salvation through Jesus Christ alone, 3) his request

---

10 A personal evangelist should consider creating an email address and registering for a Google Voice number (www.google.com/voice). He can use the new email address and virtual phone number in lieu of his personal email address and phone number. The new contact information will provide an intermediary step of security for the evangelist.

for God to forgive his sins, and 4) his gratitude for God's grace to him in a prayer. If he indicates he needs assistance in praying, instruct him to pray the previous four aspects (taking time after each one to allow him to do so) in his own words, rather than having him repeat your words after you.

2. If he previously misunderstood what he said he wanted to do but realizes he is not prepared to repent and believe, then encourage him to consider what you have told him, and leave with him a gospel tract containing contact information.

3. If he says he understands the decision, but you are unsure, then reemphasize the high demands of the gospel. If he then becomes unsure about repenting and believing, follow-up with discerning questions to determine how, or if, the Holy Spirit is working conviction in his heart that leads to repentance. However, if upon hearing the high demands of the gospel and under the conviction of the Holy Spirit, he remains confident about his desire to repent and believe, then do not prevent him from calling on the Lord for salvation.

CHAPTER 2

Spiritually Ripened Fields

The Harvest—a short film that tells the real-life, inspiring story of a family on a North Dakota farm—opens with a father and his three young sons surveying wheat fields stretching as far as the eye can see. The father explains to these would-be farmer boys, "By the end of the summer, the wheat will be ripened and the harvest will be ready to reap. When the harvest is ready, we must be ready, or we'll lose the whole crop."

A few weeks later the father dies unexpectedly, leaving the looming harvest behind for his grieving wife and three boys. The oldest son remembers his dad saying they would have to be ready when the harvest was ready or they would lose the entire crop. The burden of responsibility bears down on his shoulders, and he doesn't want to let his father's labors go to waste. He can't lose the crop, but even the best efforts of both his brothers and himself will not be enough to prevent it from happening. Their everyday chores are more than enough work for them. The three boys pray that God would send them help. With every day, the weather gets hotter, causing the wheat to ripen sooner than anyone expected. The day suddenly comes when the wheat is ready to be harvested, but the boys simply are not ready for it.

The oldest son wakes early in the morning, realizing the urgency of the task—how today is just one day closer to the day they will lose the harvest. After dressing, eating, and beginning his morning chores, he hears a growing roar and rumbling in the distance. As he looks, he can hardly believe his eyes. Huge combines, one after another, make their way into the harvest fields. It is as if the whole world has come to harvest the crop! Neighboring farmers begin harvesting the wheat in the big northern field until they finish the one in the south. Side by side they move from field to field, leaving a path of the work they have finished behind them.

As the oldest son watches them unload the golden wheat, he remembers his father and his own prayers for help with the harvest after his father's death. Then he understands—he wasn't alone. These people had work of their own, but they left their own fields to come and help his family. Together they did what no one could do on his own—they brought in an entire harvest in one day. The boys' prayers had been answered! The harvest was finished—the fields were clean—and the wheat was saved!

Jesus uses agricultural language, including a white, wheat-ripened field to represent spiritual truths on various occasions. When sending out His disciples (Matt 9:37-38; Luke 10:2) and responding to His disciples' curiosity when He did not eat food they had brought him (John 4:34-38), our Lord directs their eyes to a ripened, white harvest of weary people ready to believe in Him. Laborers would be necessary in order to reap the spiritual harvest, so Jesus directs His followers in Matthew 9:37-38 and Luke 10:2 to pray that the Lord of the harvest would send them. In John 4:34-38, He commands them to reap the spiritually ripened field in which others had labored. In light of these passages, consider the following reflections concerning our Lord's commands and the spiritually ripened field comprised of unbelievers.

THE SPIRITUALLY RIPENED FIELD AWAITS REAPING

Jesus describes the "field" of unbelievers as both "plentiful" (Matt 9:37-38; Luke 10:2) and "white" (John 4:34-38), indicating it is ripe and awaits reaping. In other words, Jesus tells His disciples that numerous unbelievers stand prepared to believe in Him and to repent of their sins. Although disciples who labor in a spiritually ripened field do not possess a guarantee to reap a harvest each time they work the field, they can be assured that 1) unbelievers across the globe are prepared to believe in Jesus as Savior and Lord right now and 2) their labors in the field sometimes prepare the crop for future ripening so that in due time others may be able reap it (cf., John 4:38). The work of the Spirit and the labors of past personal evangelists have resulted in today's spiritually ripened field, and today's evangelistic seed-casting cultivates a spiritually ripened field for the future.

Although we must prepare for future evangelistic endeavors, we also must remember that people readily willing to believe in Jesus and to repent of their sins cannot do so apart from hearing the gospel proclaimed (Rom 10:14).

THE SPIRITUALLY RIPENED FIELD DEMANDS URGENCY

Jesus' description of the fields being "white for harvest" implies a demand for urgency. Even an agricultural novice understands that no particular field or crop remains ripened indefinitely. Christ's depiction of a whitened harvest reminds an evangelistic harvester that any conversation or encounter he has with an unbeliever potentially could be that person's last opportunity to respond to the gospel call.

Laborers for the Lord of the harvest must not assume spiritually ripened unbelievers are independently or automatically reaped into the Lord's harvest. The notion that unbelievers obtain faith in Christ unconsciously is foreign to the Scriptures. In fact, immediately after Jesus identifies the fields as ready for reaping in John 4:35, John records, "Many Samaritans from that town believed in him because of the woman's testimony. … And many more believed because of his word" (John 4:39). Note that the Samaritans' salvation did not occur solely on the basis that they were spiritually ripened. Rather, the overwhelming number of Samaritans who believed did so *after* hearing the testimony of the Samaritan woman and Jesus' word, not *automatically* on the basis of their own meritorious receptivity.

Because of life's brevity, numerous unbelievers have limited time remaining to believe the gospel and repent of their sins. The spiritually ripened field will not be the same tomorrow as it is today. With every new day, evangelistic harvesters will observe certain field crops having been lost forever to death. Therefore, laborers for the Lord of the harvest must possess evangelistic urgency each hour of every day.

THE SPIRITUALLY RIPENED FIELD RECEIVES REAPERS THROUGH PRAYER

In both Matthew 9:37-38 and Luke 10:2, Jesus instructs His disciples to pray to the Lord of the harvest for laborers. In particular, Matthew precedes his account of this instruction by mentioning Jesus' deep compassion for helpless and harassed people. Instead of prompting anxiety about the situation among His disciples, He prompts them to prayer.

Jesus informs His disciples that prayer-prompted harvesters are necessary in order for the plenteous fields to be reaped.

Our Lord leaves the work of His evangelistic enterprise neither to coincidence nor to convenience. In addition, He does not promote a strategy of lobbying, begging, or shaming others into evangelistic enlistment. Entrusting the reaping of spiritually ripened fields neither to chance nor to campaigns, the Lord of the harvest commands His disciples to pray for the mass deployment of evangelistic laborers to reap His harvest.

THE SPIRITUALLY RIPENED FIELD REQUIRES MORE THAN PRAYER

Responsibility for harvesting the spiritually ripened field belongs to the believers of Jesus. As previously mentioned, part of the responsibility believers assume is that of praying for the enlistment of harvest laborers. However, earnest intercession to the Lord of the harvest requires more than prayer alone. No one will ever pray for evangelistic laborers without also realizing his own urgent, evangelistic responsibility to join the endeavor.

One never needs to question whether a prayer to the Lord of the harvest for evangelistic laborers falls outside the rubric of God's will. Likewise, one never needs to doubt whether the Lord of the harvest will answer such a prayer. Inevitably, the Holy Spirit prompts us to become answers to our own prayers in this regard.

In a different context perhaps you have heard someone remark, "Well, all we can do is pray." Usually someone responds this way when the situation or circumstance appears so overwhelming that they feel powerless to act. However, if a believer prays for evangelistic harvesters to be sent into the spiritually ripened field, he should expect to testify soon thereafter, "Prayer for laborers to enter the spiritually ripened field has prompted me to do all I can do!"

CONCLUSION

The Lottie Moon Christmas Offering for International Missions reminds most Southern Baptists of the global, spiritually ripened field when they are asked to give to support laborers. In his book, *Send the Light: Lottie Moon's Letters and Other Writings*, Dr. Keith Harper includes a letter Lottie Moon wrote on November 4, 1875, to the Foreign Mission Board (now the International Mission Board of the Southern Baptist

Convention). In addition to the previous reflections concerning what the Scriptures teach about the spiritually ripened field, may we all consider and act upon Lottie Moon's plea to Southern Baptists of her day about the spiritually ripened field requiring prayer-prompted harvesters:

> The harvest is plenteous, the laborers are few. ... What we find missionaries can do in the way of preaching the gospel even in the immediate neighborhood of this city is but as the thousandth part of a drop in the bucket compared with what should be done. I do not pretend to aver [claim] that there is any spiritual interest among the people. They literally "sit in darkness and in the shadow of death." The burden of our words to them is folly and sin of idol worship. We are but doing pioneer work, but breaking up the soil in which we believe others shall sow a bountiful crop. But, as in the natural soil, four or five laborers cannot possibly cultivate a radius of twenty miles, so cannot we, a mission of five people, do more than make a beginning of what should be done. ... But is there no way to arouse the churches on this subject? We missionaries find it in our hearts to say to them in all humility, "Now then we are ambassadors for Christ; as though God did beseech you by us, we pray you, in Christ's stead," to remember the heathen. We implore you to send us help. Let not these heathen sink down into eternal death without one opportunity to hear that blessed gospel which is to you the source of all joy & comfort.

Lottie Moon's words are as true today as the day she wrote them more than 100 years ago. Though she is dead, she still speaks. Shall we who remain be stirred to enter the global mission field? Shall we who remain sow gospel seed where she and others have broken the soil? Shall we who remain reap the spiritually ripened crop? The Lord of the Harvest awaits our urgent prayers for laborers, and He awaits our urgent, evangelistic labors.

CHAPTER 3

Is it Biblical to Pray for the Salvation of Unbelievers?

God has honored, and in many instances has answered, the fervent prayers of believers for the salvation of unbelievers. Concerning his own salvation, L.R. Scarborough, the second president of Southwestern Baptist Theological Seminary and inaugural occupant of the first established chair of evangelism in the world ("The Chair of Fire"), recounted:

> The human beginning of the influence leading to my salvation was in the prayer of my mother in my behalf when I was an infant. She climbed out of bed, having gone down toward the grave that I might live, and crawled on her knees across the floor to my little cradle when I was three weeks of age, and prayed that God would save me in His good time and call me to preach.[1]

In fact, research has revealed in the last two decades that regardless of their sizes or locations, Southern Baptist churches that report the highest rates of baptisms attribute praying for the salvation of unbelievers by name to their evangelistic effectiveness.[2]

---

1   L.R. Scarborough, "The Evolution of a Cowboy," in *L.R. Scarborough Collection*, 17, Archives, A. Webb Roberts Library, Southwestern Baptist Theological Seminary, Fort Worth, Texas, n.d, 1.

2   Thom Rainer, *Effective Evangelistic Churches* (Nashville: Broadman & Holman, 1996), 67–71, 76–79 and Steve R. Parr, Steve Foster, David Harrill, and Tom Crites, *Georgia's Top Evangelistic Churches: Ten Lessons from the Most Effective Churches* (Duluth: Georgia Baptist Convention, 2008), 10–11, 26, 29.

Although historical examples and investigative evidence of God's blessing on believers' prayers for the salvation of the lost can be documented, do any biblical precedents exist concerning praying for the salvation of unbelievers to substantiate these examples and evidences? Yes, the Bible does in fact establish precedence for believers to pray for the salvation of the lost, especially when one considers that Jesus practiced, Paul acknowledged, and Scripture instructs prayer for the salvation of unbelievers.

THE EXAMPLE OF JESUS

The Bible attests that Christ prayed for the lost. Concerning the suffering Servant of the Lord, Isaiah writes: "Therefore I will divide Him a portion with the great, And He shall divide the spoil with the strong, Because He poured out His soul unto death, And He was numbered with the transgressors, And He bore the sin of many, *And made intercession for the transgressors*" (Is 53:12, NKJV, emphasis added). In his account of the death of Jesus, Luke confirms that He interceded on behalf of those who crucified and reviled Him. He writes:

> And when they had come to the place called Calvary, there they crucified Him, and the criminals, one on the right hand and the other on the left. *Then Jesus said*, *"Father, forgive them, for they do not know what they do."* And they divided His garments and cast lots. And the people stood looking on. But even the rulers with them sneered, saying, "He saved others; let Him save Himself if He is the Christ, the chosen of God." The soldiers also mocked Him, coming and offering Him sour wine, and saying, "If You are the King of the Jews, save Yourself" (Luke 23:33-36, NKJV, emphasis added).

As Christ suffered for the sins of the world on the cross, He prayed for the forgiveness of sinners who crucified and reviled Him. The Bible does not indicate that all, or even many, of those for whose forgiveness He prayed actually received it. Nevertheless, one of the crucified criminals who at first derided Him (Matt 27:44) later entreated the Lord. As a result, he was forgiven of his sins and naturalized a citizen of Paradise by the Savior who cared enough to pray for him.

THE ACKNOWLEDGMENT OF PAUL

In addition, the apostle Paul acknowledged praying for the salvation of unbelieving Israel. He wrote to the believers in Rome, "Brethren, my heart's desire and prayer to God for Israel is that they may be saved" (Rom 10:1, NKJV). Paul's desire for the salvation of his fellow countrymen led him to pray for their salvation. Although not all Israel was saved during his lifetime, he looked forward in faith to a day when the fullness of the Gentiles' salvation would be accomplished and his prayer for Israel to be saved would be answered (Rom 11:26a).

THE INSTRUCTION OF SCRIPTURE

Finally, believers are commanded to pray in various ways for all people, kings, and authorities. Paul writes,

> Therefore I exhort first of all that supplications, prayers, intercessions, and giving of thanks be made for all men, for kings and all who are in authority, that we may lead a quiet and peaceable life in all godliness and reverence. For this is good and acceptable in the sight of God our Savior, who desires all men to be saved and to come to the knowledge of the truth (1 Tim 2:1-4, NKJV).

The apostle explains that the prescribed petitions on behalf of "all men, ... kings ... [and those] who are in authority" 1) should be practiced in order to live godly and reverently in peace and 2) should prove good and acceptable to God who desires the salvation of everyone. For these reasons, the supplications, prayers, and intercessions required of believers should include a petition for the salvation of all people.

Consider that most, if not all, of the kings and authorities to whom Paul refers were not only nonbelievers, but they had actively oppressed believers. No wonder Paul appeals to the hope of a day when believers could lead godly and reverent lives in peace, free from the threat of persecution. Such a day was possible if the believers in Paul's day would pray for the salvation of these tyrannical rulers, and as a result of hearing the gospel they would believe, thus bringing an end to their oppressiveness.

In addition, Paul claims that praying for the salvation of all men is pleasing and acceptable to God. As Thomas Lea explains, "The relative clause of v. 4 provides the basis for the assertion in v. 3 that prayer for all people is pleasing to God. The goal of the prayers Paul urged is that all people be saved. *Intercession for all people pleases the God who desires all to be saved.*[3] God desires to see everyone saved and come to the knowledge of the truth, though not all will do so.

Therefore, in order to lead godly and reverent lives in peace and to please God with their supplication, prayers, and intercession, believers are instructed to pray for the salvation of all people, great and small.

CONCLUSION

In a sermon he entitled, *Mary Magdalene*, C.H. Spurgeon urged the following in regards to believers' responsibility to plead for the salvation of the lost:

> Until the gate of hell is shut upon a man, we must not cease to pray for him. And if we see him hugging the very doorposts of damnation, we must go to the mercy seat and beseech the arm of grace to pluck him from his dangerous position. While there is life there is hope, and although the soul is almost smothered with despair, we must not despair for it, but rather arouse ourselves to awaken the Almighty arm.[4]

On their own merit, historical examples like that of Scarborough and/or pragmatic evidences like those documented by Rainer and Parr provide believers reasons to pray for the salvation of unbelievers. However, the example of Jesus, the acknowledgement of Paul, and the instruction of 1 Timothy 2:1-4 as presented above reveal to believers their obligation to pray for the salvation of the lost.

When a believer prays for the soul of a lost person and he is subsequently saved, skeptics may attribute it to nothing more than mere coincidence. When churches pray for the salvation of unbelievers by name and effective evangelistic growth results, cynics might consider it pragmatism. However, perhaps the most appropriate label to designate believers who pray for the salvation of the lost would be "biblical."

---

3   Thomas D. Lea and Hayne P. Griffin Jr. 1, 2 *Timothy, Titus*, The New American Commentary, vol. 34 (Nashville: Broadman & Holman, 1992), 89 [emphasis added].
4   C.H. Spurgeon, "Mary Magdalene," Sermon No. 792, January 26, 1868.

CHAPTER 4

Soil-Speculative or Soul-Driven Evangelism?

Accompanying your father on a fishing trip brings fond memories to mind; that is, as long as he isn't always catching more fish than you. I have the "blessing," as Dad calls it, or the "curse," as I refer to it, of having a father who always catches more fish than I. During the first weekend of almost every June, my father wastes no time demonstrating this fact when he and I go trout fishing on the Tuckaseegee River in Jackson County, North Carolina.

Every year it's the same routine: I find a particular place in the river I'm convinced is teeming with fish, so I spend the entire morning there and catch very few fish, if any at all. On the other hand, Dad wastes no time at any one particular place. He casts the bait on his pole in one place no more than three or four times and continues that process until his bait locates a place in the river where fish are swarming. Each year dad knows he'll find me in the place where he saw me last. And inevitably he catches more fish than I, continually offering me the same advice: "Son, cast your bait all along the river and let it, not your hunches about the holes, bring in the catch." After years of "speculative" fishing, I'm convinced now to use my bait to test the reliability of my hunches.

Jesus likens, or refers to, evangelism as "fishing for men" (Matt 4:19, 13:47-50; Mark 1:17). Evangelism seems to be in mind also when He delivers His parable of a sower sowing seed (Matt 13:1-9, 18-23; Mark

4:1-9, 14-20; Luke 8:4-8, 11-15). Using these two metaphors can help Christians evaluate our methods of evangelism as well as our expectations of the result.

In the parable, Jesus likens the gospel, or the "word of the kingdom," to the sower's seed. Broadcast by the sower, the seed falls either along the pathway, upon rocky ground, among thorns, or on good soil. Some disagreement exists among commentators about the kinds of responses these four soil types represent. However, Jesus' explanation of the parable seems to suggest that the three former types of soil indicate people's eventual failure to respond to the gospel's invitation, while the latter soil denotes those who understand and gladly receive the gospel.

When preaching Matthew 13:3-23 a few years ago, Dr. Steven Smith, vice president and professor of communications at Southwestern Seminary, keenly remarked, "It is only when someone is exposed to the seed do they [or you] know what type of soil they are, and if we're not preaching the gospel to people, they [or you] don't have any way to judge who they are."[1] Believing that gospel seed manifests the type of response each person makes upon a particular time he hears the gospel, a personal evangelist should base the frequency of his evangelism upon his complete confidence in the "seed" of the gospel rather than personal conjecture about the "soil" of someone's anticipated response.

At some time or another, a personal evangelist will doubtless be tempted to base his decision to evangelize someone on his own impressions and/or speculation of that person's likelihood to profess or reject Christ at a given moment. He must resist this temptation for at least two reasons.

1. The Parable of the Sower (Matt 13:1-9, 18-23; Mark 4:1–9, 14-20; Luke 8:4-8, 11-15) does not substantiate soil-speculative evangelism. The sower-evangelist of these texts scatters the gospel seed indiscriminately and generously, not theoretically or hypothetically.

2. Yielding to the temptation of evangelizing only those who appear ready to respond is ultimately an attempt to access omniscience only available to God. One of the many ways Scripture attests to Jesus' divinity can be found in His ability to perceive the hearts and minds of others (*cf.*, Matt 9:3–4;

---

1   Steven Smith, "The Gospel has a Future;" accessed on May 8, 2014, http://swbts.edu/media/ item/145/swbts-chapel-october-13-2010.

Mark 2:6–8; Luke 5:21–22, 24:38; John 1:45–50, 2:24–25, 5:42, 6:61, 64). Only God, not a perceptive personal evangelist, possesses the omniscient and intimate knowledge of how anyone, at any time, will respond to a gospel appeal.

The Parable of the Sower reminds personal evangelists that sowers scatter seed; they do not inspect soils. Therefore, when "fishing for men" they must spend more time proclaiming the gospel of the kingdom than they do evaluating the likelihood of others' responses to the gospel. So instead of basing when and where you'll "fish for men" upon a personal assumption of "fishing holes" that appear to be teeming with bountiful catches, consider taking a wise father's advice: "Trust the constantly casted bait [of the gospel], not your hunches about the holes, to bring in the catch."

CHAPTER 5

Gripped by Fear? Overcoming Obstacles in Evangelism

One evening several years ago, a Maryville, Tenn., college student named George leaped out of bed, switched on his light, and shouted to his roommate, "I've got it! I've got it!" Awakened from his sleep, the roommate asked, "What have you got, George?"

George replied, "Everyone in the U.S. has a chance to hear the gospel—but not in Mexico. We should go there this summer and distribute tracts. How about it?" Stumbling over his words, the roommate said, "Well, George, I don't know. I'd have to pray about it."

"Okay, let's pray," said George as he knelt beside his bed. A couple of minutes later, George lifted his head and asked, "So, are you ready to go now?" The roommate was reluctant to finalize a commitment to go so far, so soon. George muttered, "It takes some people so long to decide to do anything!" Years later, George Verwer, this evangelistic college student, became the founder of Operation Mobilization.

Like Verwer's roommate, believers in Jesus Christ often experience obstacles to the personal discipline of evangelism. Many of these obstacles arise from issues related to fear. Consider the following obstacles to evangelism and some ways you can overcome them.

1. FEAR OF THE UNKNOWN IMPEDES BELIEVERS' EVANGELISM BY EMPHASIZING UNFAMILIAR EXPERIENCES.

Some believers do not evangelize because they do not know what to expect if they were to share the gospel with others. Perhaps they are unsure who might be inside the houses they are to visit. Maybe they are uncertain about the reaction they will receive from those sitting nearby at the local coffee shop or from unbelieving friends.

Regarding the fear of the unknown, every believer has a choice—either allow the unknown to remain mysterious by not evangelizing, or make known the unknown by evangelizing. A believer will never know what will or will not happen in a particular witnessing situation if s/he does not offer others a clear and complete witness to the saving power of Jesus Christ's death, burial, and resurrection and call for a commitment. Of all the possible responses others can offer to believers who share the glorious gospel of Jesus Christ, more than likely, they will either want to hear more on the matter or politely decline the conversation.

2. FEAR FOR SAFETY HINDERS SOME BELIEVERS FROM EVANGELIZING IN AN EFFORT TOWARD SELF-PRESERVATION.

In an environment where reports of Christians' falling under attack for preaching the gospel around the globe become more and more normative, some believers naturally fear for their own safety. This news should come as no surprise to believers who follow a Savior who was despised and rejected by men to the point of death. In fact, when Jesus warned His followers of the dangers they would endure for His name's sake, He didn't excuse them from evangelizing for the sake of safety. Rather, He charged them that "the gospel must first be preached to all the nations" (*cf.* Mark 13:9–13, NKJV).

Although danger is not out of the realm of possibility, most believers in America need not fear for their safety while sharing the gospel in their own communities. Of course, all believers should exercise wisdom when witnessing (*e.g.*, not trespassing on property with clearly marked "No Trespassing" signage; not arguing with someone who disagrees with gospel premises; etc.). In fact, those who evangelize on a consistent basis generally experience few, if any, dangerous encounters when evangelizing.

3. FEAR OF REJECTION PREVENTS BELIEVERS FROM EVANGELIZING BY SHIFTING ATTENTION FROM JESUS TO THEMSELVES.

Generally speaking, most people want to be accepted by others. Some believers don't evangelize for fear that those with whom they share the gospel will reject them when they call for decisions.

Those who battle the fear of rejection should remind themselves of the words of Jesus when He said, "But whoever denies Me before men, him will I also deny before My Father who is in heaven" (Matt 10:33, NKJV). When evangelizing, believers must first convey the message that only Jesus Christ can reconcile men and women to God through His death and resurrection and then call their listeners to a commitment of believing in Jesus alone for salvation and repenting of their sins. After the gospel is clearly communicated, any rejection on the part of the evangelized is much more serious than whether or not the personal evangelist has been denied. Any denial to the clearly communicated message of the gospel is a denial of Jesus Christ Himself. On a related note, not every time a believer evangelizes can s/he be guaranteed that someone will accept Christ and His free gift of forgiveness, but a believer can be guaranteed that no one will ever accept Christ and His free gift of forgiveness if s/he never evangelizes.

4. FEAR OF FAILURE OBSTRUCTS BELIEVERS FROM SHARING THE GOSPEL BY CAUSING THEM TO ADOPT A FAULTY UNDERSTANDING OF SUCCESS.

Many believers accept the false premise that evangelism is successful only if someone makes a profession of faith in Jesus Christ for salvation. This misunderstanding, if accepted by believers, can prove devastating.

While no one will deny that a profession of faith brings great joy, encouragement, and affirmation to a personal evangelist, these results must never be equated with success. If the decisions of those who are evangelized rested solely on the abilities of believers, then perhaps professions of faith, or the lack thereof, could be categorized in terms of success or failure. However, the decisions of those who are evangelized rest with them and the work of the Holy Spirit. Believers' success and failure in terms of evangelism is measured by their obedience or disobedience to the Great Commission of Jesus Christ.

5. DREAD OF PAST NEGATIVE EVANGELISTIC EXPERIENCES PROMOTES A FEAR THAT PARALYZES SOME BELIEVERS IN THEIR EVANGELISM.

Some believers don't evangelize because they fear a repeating of previous negative evangelism experiences. Whether their own mistakes, such as forgetting a Scripture reference, or the reactions of others, these negative experiences can easily sideline formerly eager witnesses. Even the memories of negative circumstances, such as seeing no one come to the door on church visitation night, can elicit fear at the next opportunity for evangelism. Although many believers tend to let these negative experiences push them into evangelistic paralysis, they should instead evaluate and learn from the experiences in order to emerge stronger and ready for the next encounter.

6. FEAR OF EMULATING PERCEIVED MANIPULATION IN OTHERS' EVANGELISM FOSTERS A DESIRE TO OVERCORRECT BY NOT EVANGELIZING AT ALL.

While some believers let their own negative experiences paralyze them, others focus on the perceived manipulation of others to excuse themselves from evangelizing. They cite examples of manipulative attempts at evangelism, and they overcorrect by not evangelizing at all. In reality, however, manipulation is a matter of the heart much more than it is a matter of practice. By guarding their own hearts, these believers can minimize their risk of manipulating others, who desperately need to hear the gospel proclaimed to them personally.

7. FEAR OF PERCEIVED FANATICISM PROMOTES WITHIN BELIEVERS AN AVERSION TO EVANGELIZE.

Other potential evangelists fail to share the gospel because they do not want hearers to call them "fanatics." In truth, obedient believers almost always face ridicule for acting on their love for Christ, but they should remember that this ridicule generally stems from misunderstanding, jealousy, or guilt. With their eyes on Christ, they must echo the apostles' determination to obey God rather than man (Acts 4:19-20). Concern about the opinions of others will fade in the light of Christ's approval.

8. AN ABSENCE OF THE FEAR OF GOD STRIPS BELIEVERS OF A HEALTHY MOTIVATION TO EVANGELIZE THE LOST.

To this point in the discussion, believers have been encouraged to shun fear in terms of obstacles to evangelism. However, all believers must embrace the fear of God, especially in terms of their witness for Christ.

The apostle Paul wrote, "Knowing therefore the terror [fear] of the Lord, we persuade men. . . Now then, we are ambassadors for Christ, as though God were pleading through us: we implore you on Christ's behalf, be reconciled to God" (2 Cor 5:11, 20, NKJV). In his commentary on 2 Corinthians in the *New American Commentary* series, David Garland explains that terror (*e.g.*, fear) here refers to "a religious consciousness, a reverential awe of God, that directs the way one lives"[1]. Believers' consistently living devoid of the fear of God, at best, will end in forfeiture of heavenly rewards and, at worst, will generate apathy for the lost.

Aware of the day he would appear before the *bema* seat of Christ (2 Cor 5:10), Paul seeks to persuade, implore, and plead with others to be reconciled to God by proclaiming the gospel of Jesus Christ. Believers must fear God because they, like Paul, will one day stand before the *bema* seat of our Lord and give account for what they have and have not done during their lives, which includes the extent of their faithfulness in evangelism. Christ's judgment at the *bema* seat will result either in receiving or in forfeiting heavenly, eternal rewards.

Much more urgent than what heavenly rewards believers will or will not receive, the fear of God reminds personal evangelists of His impending wrath and judgment upon unbelievers. While believers will appear before the *bema* seat of Christ, all unbelievers will appear before the Great White Throne to be judged and condemned (Rev 20:11–15). Those who appear at this judgment will be punished eternally in hell because they have neglected to respond in faith and repentance to Jesus Christ. Believers must embrace the fear of God and evangelize in order to avoid an uncompassionate apathy for the final state of the lost.

Doubtless, all believers at some time or another face one or more of these fear-related obstacles to evangelism. The two primary and greatest catalysts to overcome fear-related obstacles to one's personal practice of evangelism include the convicting power of the Word of God and the

---

1   David Garland, *2 Corinthians,* New American Commentary (Nashville: B&H, 1999), 269-270.

empowering ability of the Holy Spirit. As you read the Bible for conviction and pray for divine empowerment in order to conquer obstacles in evangelism, consider identifying which of the fear-related obstacles threaten your evangelistic faithfulness and applying the particular suggestions offered above that address them.

George Verwer was known to encourage others to evangelize with the impassioned plea, "We are God's chosen people, not his frozen people, so let's pray for defrost!" May fear-related obstacles no longer freeze beautiful feet in their tracks from proclaiming the good news of Jesus Christ for salvation.

CHAPTER 6

Finding Evangelistic Confidence

Instead of seeking after the lost, many believers spend time searching for the confidence to evangelize. They tell themselves, "If only I had more confidence, I would share the gospel with my friends and acquaintances that I know need Christ." Imagine how much confidence they believe they would need to share Christ with someone who is hostile to the gospel.

In the middle of the last century, a rodeo clown and steer wrestler named Ken Boen lived in Fort Smith, Ark. Boen was hostile to the gospel and had a reputation in the area as the last person in the world who would ever receive Christ. A number of pastors, evangelists, and lay people attempted to share the gospel with him, and he invariably rejected their offers to receive Christ. In fact, almost no believer in Fort Smith had any confidence when it came to evangelizing Boen because of the hardness of his heart.

Have you ever been in need of evangelistic confidence? Every believer, at some time or another, has needed evangelistic confidence. One way personal evangelists have found confidence over the years has been to enroll in evangelism training. Evangelism training has provided willing evangelists confidence by teaching them a gospel script that they can memorize, so they would know what to say when they evangelized.

While evangelism training provides willing evangelists with confidence to know what to say when they evangelize, it does not necessarily always give them confidence to begin evangelistic conversations. How, then, do evangelists find the confidence to share the gospel with those who are open to hear it as well as with those who are hostile against it?

Consider the evangelistic confidence of Peter and John as recorded in Acts 4:13-20.

Having healed a lame man in the name of Jesus (3:1-10), Peter and John were preaching the resurrection from the dead through Jesus in Jerusalem (3:11-26; 4:1-2). The priests, the captain of the temple guard, and the Sadducees took offense and arrested them (4:1-3). Nevertheless, 5,000 of those who heard their message believed on Jesus (4:4).

The next day, the apostles were put on trial and asked by their accusers, "By what power, or in what name, have you done this?" (4:5-7, NASB). With complete confidence and filled with the Holy Spirit, Peter responded that they had done this in the name of Jesus Christ the Nazarene (4:8-12). Then, Acts 4:13-20 records:

> Now as they *observed the confidence* of Peter and John and *understood that they were uneducated and untrained men, they were amazed, and began to recognize them as having been with Jesus*. And seeing the man who had been healed standing with them, they had nothing to say in reply. But when they had ordered them to leave the Council, they began to confer with one another, saying, "What shall we do with these men? For the fact that a noteworthy miracle has taken place through them is apparent to all who live in Jerusalem, and we cannot deny it. But so that it will not spread any further among the people, let us warn them to speak no longer to any man in this name." And when they had summoned them, they commanded them not to speak or teach at all in the name of Jesus. *But Peter and John answered and said to them, "Whether it is right in the sight of God to give heed to you rather than to God, you be the judge; for we cannot stop speaking about what we have seen and heard"* (NASB, emphasis mine).

Notice that the members of the Sanhedrin in amazement observed Peter and John's confidence in spite of the fact that they were both uneducated and untrained men. They attributed the apostles' confidence to the fact that they had been with Jesus.

If believers have known enough of the gospel to be saved by it, then they will know enough of the gospel to share it with others. However, evangelistic confidence is not attained merely by what believers know (such as a memorized, evangelistic script); it is attained by Whom they know (Jesus Christ).

Many believers today have received more evangelism training than those in the early church did. How, then, did early believers know what to say when they evangelized? What was the secret of their evangelistic confidence? They were with Jesus (4:13). They remembered what they had seen (4:20). They recalled what they had heard (4:20). Those seeking evangelistic confidence will find it whenever they spend time with Jesus. Those who spend time with Jesus cannot help but spend time telling others about Jesus. In addition, those with whom we spend time telling about Jesus can tell whether or not we spend time with Jesus (4:13).

Well-known evangelist J. Harold Smith came to serve as the pastor of the First Baptist Church of Fort Smith, Ark., in 1953. J. Harold Smith was a man who walked with God because he, like Peter and John, confidently told almost everyone with whom he came into contact about Jesus Christ. Not long after assuming his new pastorate, Smith heard about Ken Boen. Despite Boen's reputation of having a hardened heart to the gospel, Smith paid him a visit him at his home. He wasn't confident that Boen would receive Christ, but he was confident that Jesus would be with him when he went.

Dressed in his best Sunday suit and shoes, Smith gingerly stepped around and over the mud puddles to meet Boen, who was in the field, tending to his horses. Boen listened to the pastor-evangelist as he shared the gospel with him. Smith then asked him if he would be willing to receive Jesus Christ as His Lord and Savior. Boen's eyes scanned the preacher from his head to his feet, looked at the mud puddles all around his feet, and then peered deeply into Smith's eyes. He replied, "Preacher, if you're willing to bend down on your knees with me to pray right now, then I'm willing to receive Christ right now." With no hesitation at all, Smith confidently bent down in the mud. Though the evangelist's clean suit and shoes became a muddy mess, the steer wrestler's filthy heart was made clean as he, himself, bent to his knees and received Jesus Christ as his Savior and Lord.

May we display such boldness and confidence in sharing the Gospel as we spend time with Jesus.

CHAPTER 7

What's Your Method? Advice about Evangelistic Approaches

Most Christians recognize the importance of evangelism, but they are at a loss when it comes to striking up a conversation with a stranger on a plane, in a grocery line, or at the gas station. The following chapter analyzes six common approaches to sharing the gospel and includes some additional evangelism tips. Each approach has potential strengths and weaknesses, but not all approaches are created equal. All six approaches have their own advantages and usefulness in particular situations; therefore, effective personal evangelists will learn how to utilize more than one of these approaches and guard against their potential weaknesses. The leading of the Holy Spirit should dictate which approach, or approaches, should be incorporated in any given evangelistic encounter.

THE CHARGING BULL

The *Charging Bull* comes out of nowhere, rushes in on an unsuspecting stranger, and launches into an evangelistic presentation before a person can get out "Hello. My name is ..." Like a bull in a china shop, he does not seek to build bridges in the conversation or to develop a relationship. He simply takes control of the conversation.

While this person can be applauded for being very direct and intentional in evangelism, this approach often forces the conversation and can lend itself to manipulation or people feeling pressured. When this happens, people will either change the subject or, worse, make a false profession of faith out of fear or ignorance just to get the bull to back off or go away. The bull also has a tendency to focus on his ability to convince the other person rather than the Holy Spirit's work to convict.

Personal evangelism occurs in the context of conversations, not monologues. Those practicing personal evangelism as though it is a one-sided conversation will see their listeners tune out for lack of interest. Everyday evangelists should present as much of the gospel as possible to their listeners, but they should also encourage feedback so that their gospel presentations can naturally address listeners' specific situations, rather than sounding canned and forced.

THE STORY TELLER

The *Story Teller* uses his testimony to present the gospel. A narrative approach is ideal when you are sitting next to someone on a plane. For example, you can ask him if he is coming or going, make small talk, and ask him what he does for a living. Typically, as the conversation progresses, the person will ask you about yourself. At this point, you should share with them a little about your family and what you do and attempt to bridge the conversation into an opportunity to share your testimony.

Sharing your testimony is a strong approach because it is natural and relational. However, one weakness to this approach is that we sometimes get bogged down in sharing our story, and then the conversation either gets sidetracked or never contains an explicit explanation of the gospel.

In order to overcome this outcome, believers should have a three-part mental outline prepared: 1) what life was like before Christ; 2) how you came to Christ; and 3) what your life has been like since coming to Christ. Be careful not to spend the majority of the time on your life before Christ or after Christ. You want to spend the most time on how you came to Christ as you mix in an explicit gospel presentation.

THE INQUISITOR

The *Inquisitor* asks questions that lead the conversation to a point where he can directly share the gospel. Jesus best modeled this questioning approach, such as in his conversation with the woman at the well. Randy Newman's book *Questioning Evangelism* is an excellent resource for those interested in learning more about this approach.

One potential weakness with this approach is that the person may feel defensive if you bombard him with too many questions. Additionally, when you ask an extrovert a series of questions, he might dominate the conversation with his answers, leaving you no time to share the gospel.

To avoid these dangers, believers should stick to a brief set of questions that are direct and thought out. Avoid general, open-ended questions. You will want to have in mind a blueprint in which you can drive the conversation straight to the death of Christ and His resurrection from the dead.

THE ANALOGIST

The *Analogist* utilizes his environment, circumstances, situations, and current events to lead a conversation to the gospel. It could be talking to your doctor about the Great Physician or connecting a news story to evil or hopelessness in the world.

Of course, one liability to this approach is that it may sound like a good connection in your mind but come off cheesy. Another hazard is that you could end up arguing about opposing political or economic views and never have the chance to get to the gospel. However, the strength in this approach is that it is natural, conversational, and effective in bridging to the gospel.

THE SERVER

The *Server* serves others through either planned or spontaneous acts of service in order to create an opportunity to evangelize another. Examples include servanthood evangelism, mercy ministries, and random acts of kindness. This approach demonstrates compassion and concern on behalf of the evangelist for the other person(s).

While personal evangelists must demonstrate genuine concern for unbelievers, this approach has the potential to lead them to adopt some unwise evangelism philosophies and practices. For example, some *Servers* will convince themselves that they must earn a right to evangelize a stranger. Attempting to earn a right to evangelize can foster a *quid pro quo* kind of evangelism, in which personal evangelists foster an expectation that those who receive their acts of service must listen to their gospel presentations or feel guilty for not doing so. *Servers* who adopt this philosophy and practice should remind themselves that as Lord, Jesus has "earned" the right to command us to adopt the biblical philosophy and practice of evangelizing as many as possible, as soon as possible.

Over time, other well-meaning *Servers* will follow the path of social gospel advocates by confusing benevolence with evangelism or by promoting an unhealthy interdependence between gospel proclamation and mercy ministry. Believers have an obligation to practice both gospel proclamation and mercy ministry without the self-imposed guilt or expectation that they must do one in order to do the other.

Jesus, who healed many infirmities and provided food for multitudes' hunger, stated that He came "to seek and save that which was lost" (Matt 18:11; Luke 19:10). If evangelism is relegated to nothing more than the practice of social services to those in need, then many people, including atheists, Muslims, Hindus, and Buddhists, evangelize. If this is the case (and it's not!), then it follows that they, too, have the gospel. Everyday evangelists should practice compassion, even meet physical needs when possible, as they evangelize, but they should prioritize the practice of biblical evangelism as they alone can offer the Bread of Life (John 6:31-35, 48, 50-51, 58).

Last, *Servers* will want to be prepared to practice other evangelistic approaches, as well. If they do not, they will find that they only evangelize those who have needs they, themselves, can meet. Those utilizing the *Server* approach and no other approach(es) must be reminded that Jesus died to save those who have no discernible physical needs (*e.g.*, the rich), as well as those who have needs greater than *Servers* can meet. *Servers* have a responsibility to proclaim the gospel to these groups, too!

THE NETWORKER

In his desire to be incarnational, the *Networker* meets and befriends others with the intent to evangelize them. The relational nature between the evangelist and the other person(s) allows for further discussion of questions about the gospel, demonstrates for the other person a Christian lifestyle, and fosters a relationship that will prove helpful for subsequent discipleship if the other person professes faith in Christ.

Networkers will be tempted to delay evangelizing their newfound friends for fear of a negative effect on the relationships they seek to establish. Southwestern Seminary pastoral ministry professor Tommy Kiker tells the story of a missionary who left America to live in another country. Almost immediately, he made friends with one of the citizens; however, he assumed that his new friend was not ready to hear the gospel. After several months, the missionary was reassigned and scheduled a meeting with his friend to say goodbye. The missionary looked deeply into the eyes of his friend and said, "I have bad news. The company for which I work has relocated me, so I will have to leave. Over the last several month, I have grown to love you as a dear friend, so before I leave I want to share with you the most important thing I could ever share with you." The friend stopped the missionary and said, "If what you have to share is so important, then why didn't you share it with me earlier?"

Personal evangelists in the New Testament do not make friends with a stranger in order to tell them about Christ after a period of time. Rather, they share Christ with strangers and as a result relationships, usually in the context of a local church, are established.

Also, *Networkers* should be careful in any attempt to prepare new acquaintances to hear the gospel after a "sufficient" level of trust (however that can be measured) has been established. Such an attempt can lead would-be evangelists to emphasize relationship-building to the neglect of acknowledging both the Holy Spirit's preparing unbelievers' hearts to receive the gospel and the uncertainty of future encounters. For example, how can evangelists know to what extent the Holy Spirit has prepared others' hearts to receive the message of the gospel if they have not shared the gospel with them (*cf.* Matt 13:1-9, 18-23)? What certainty do evangelists have that they will be able to meet with their new acquaintances/friends long enough to build a "sufficient" level of trust in order to share the gospel with them? What if their new acquaintances/friends do not want to ever meet again? What if they die before "sufficient" trust is built? What if Jesus returns before they hear the gospel?

SOME ADVICE FOR IMPROVING YOUR PERSONAL EVANGELISM

After identifying your natural approach(es) to evangelism and safeguarding yourself against their potential pitfalls, the following tips should assist you as you practice everyday evangelism:

- **Be intentional about starting conversations with people in public.** Get in the habit of speaking to strangers and making small talk.

- **If you struggle with motivation or fear, ask yourself this question:** "Am I willing to take the chance that someone else either has in the past or will in the future share the gospel with this person?" You may not know his past or future conversations, but you can be sure that he will hear it now if you speak.

- **Always carry a gospel tract.** If the person seems disinterested, the conversation gets interrupted, or you share the gospel and he does not respond, you can always leave the tract with him to read at a later time.

- **Always call for a response to the gospel.** No gospel presentation is complete without inviting the person to repent of his sin and place his faith in Christ.

- **Always offer to pray for the person.** Prayer often opens doors to an evangelistic conversation even with someone who might otherwise seem disinterested.

CHAPTER 8

I Question Your Evangelism!

A lady once criticized the evangelism methods used by Dwight L. Moody, famed 19th-century American pastor, to win people to saving faith in the Lord Jesus Christ. In response, Moody replied, "I agree with you. I don't like the way I do it either. Tell me, how do you do it?" Moody's critic answered, "I don't do it." Moody quipped, "In that case, I like my way of doing it better than your way of not doing it."

Like Moody, I would rather be a criticized personal evangelist than a non-evangelistic critic. Sometimes another's critique of our evangelism is biblically warranted. At other times critical comments about our evangelism discourage us without cause. Perhaps the evangelistic enterprise would be served best if before 1) we critique and/or question the evangelistic practices of someone else, and/or 2) our evangelistic practices are critiqued and/or questioned by someone else, we sternly look ourselves in the mirror and say, "I question your evangelism!"

What questions might a believer ask himself in order to assess his evangelistic practices? In *Tell It Often–Tell It Well*, Mark McCloskey offers three essential questions every believer should ask himself in order to assess his evangelism and its methods biblically. In addition to McCloskey's three questions (which are enumerated in the list below), I suggest five additional questions. A believer's response to each of these eight questions assists him in discerning whether or not someone else's critique of his evangelism proves warranted, and what aspects of his evangelism fall short of the biblical ideal and need adjusting.

CONCERNING YOUR PRACTICE(S) OF EVANGELISM:

1. Does the New Testament teach it?[1]

Evangelism finds its origin in the New Testament. A believer who assesses his evangelistic practices should begin by ensuring his evangelism conforms to the evangelistic doctrines, instructions, and principles found in the New Testament. McCloskey offers a few follow-up questions that frame the context of this particular question for personal evangelistic assessment. These questions include the following: "Is my approach to evangelism grounded in theological convictions regarding salvation, the gospel, and evangelism? Is it grounded in the certainties of God's plan to redeem a lost creation, the lostness of man, and responsibilities of our ambassadorship?"[2]

Concerning theological convictions regarding salvation, the gospel, and evangelism, Alvin Reid correctly states: "A conviction about a great salvation leads to a passion for evangelism."[3] However, even someone passionate for evangelism either can hold to erroneous theological convictions or alter his theological convictions over time. A believer's theological convictions concerning salvation inevitably contribute to the gospel content he presents to unbelievers. Therefore, a personal evangelist's theological convictions and the message he proclaims must be tested continually by New Testament doctrine, instructions, and principles. Because it serves as the authoritative and foundational source for evangelism, the New Testament must inform the reasons for and way(s) in which a believer evangelizes.

2. Did the first-century church demonstrate it?[4]

The first-century church initially received the Great Commission of our Lord, who passed it down to all ages of His church. For this reason, a believer interested in assessing his evangelism should consider the philosophy, practice, and pattern of the apostolic church. To assist someone in this dimension of his evangelistic assessment, McCloskey suggests the following supplemental considerations: "Has my philosophy and

---

1   Mark McCloskey, *Tell it Often-Tell it Well: Making the Most of Witnessing Opportunities* (San Bernardino: Here's Life, 1986. Reprint, Nashville: Thomas Nelson, 1995), 185.
2   Ibid.
3   Alvin Reid, *Evangelism Handbook: Biblical, Spiritual, Intentional, Missional* (Nashville: B&H, 2009), 141.
4   McCloskey, *Tell it Often-Tell it Well*, 185-186.

practice of evangelism been modeled by the first-century church? Have the theological realities that drove the first-century church to proclaim the gospel with boldness and sensitivity caused me to develop similar patterns for communicating my faith?"[5] Biblical evangelism results from one's evangelistic consistency with the philosophy, practice, and pattern of the early church.

The first-century church employed an evangelistic philosophy that endeavored to evangelize as many as possible, as quickly as possible, and as clearly as possible. Though they employed other evangelistic methods, Luke recorded numerous times in which the apostles (*e.g.*, Acts 2:12-41; 3:11-26; 4:5-12; 5:19-21), deacons (*e.g.*, Acts 6:8-7:60; 8:4-6, 12, 40), and disciples (*e.g.*, Acts 2:5-11) of the early church evangelized as many people as possible, by preaching the gospel publicly. New Testament believers do not evangelize unbelievers by both building friendships and sharing a little of the gospel over a period of time. Rather, they evangelize unbelievers by sharing complete presentations of the gospel at specific points in time (*e.g.*, John 3:1-12; 4:1-42; Acts 16:6-15; 17:16–34; 24:1-27).

Additionally, members of the first-century church also evangelized as quickly as possible. The New Testament indicates at least two reasons for the rapid rate of their evangelism. First, in order that the gospel of Jesus Christ not "*spread* any further among the people," the elders, rulers, and scribes charged Peter and John not to speak or teach in the name of Jesus (Acts 4:17-20, emphasis added). However, Peter and John claimed that they could not help but to speak of what they had seen and heard. Second, upon being brought back before the Jewish council a second time for evangelizing in the temple, the high priest questioned why Peter and John continued to "*fill* Jerusalem" with their teaching (Acts 5:27-29, emphasis added). Peter and John responded that they must obey God and not men.

In addition to its evangelistic philosophy and practice, the apostolic church also provides a pattern for evangelistic proclamation. A personal evangelist faces temptations to adopt worldly, even sinful, standards in order to gain a hearing and become relevant.[6] Nevertheless, he must be

---

5   Ibid.
6   Though not commenting on this particular temptation, Edward Rommen articulates the danger of yielding to such a temptation when he writes: "We are under great pressure to adapt the [g]ospel to its cultural surroundings. While there is a legitimate concern for contextualization, what most often happens in these cases is an outright capitulation of the [g]ospel to the principles of that culture." *Get Real: On Evangelism in the Late Modern World* (Pasadena: William Carey Library, 2010), 371.

convinced that an evangelistic lifestyle incorporates a pattern, or lifestyle, of biblical holiness. While not every evangelistic approach practiced today can be found in Scripture (for example, internet evangelism), an evangelistic practice consistent with Scripture conforms to its standards of holiness, as the first-century church practiced it.

3. Does it ground itself in the authoritative command of Jesus found in the Great Commission?

McCloskey suggests we ought not to ask ourselves, "Why are men not coming to us?" Rather we must ask ourselves, "Why are we not going to men?"[7] Though many symptoms prevent us from going to men with the gospel, they all result from disobedience to Jesus' authoritative command in the Great Commission.

In his day, William Carey confronted such disobedience when he published *An Enquiry into the Obligations of Christians to Use Means for the Conversion of the Heathens*. He described the Great Commission disobedience of believers in his day when he wrote:

> [B]ut the work has not been taken up, or prosecuted of late years (except by a few individuals) with the zeal and perseverance with which the primitive Christians went about it. It seems as if many thought the commission was sufficiently put in execution by what the apostles and others have done; that we have enough to do to attend to the salvation of our own countrymen; and that, if God intends the salvation of the heathen, he will some way or the other bring them to the gospel, or the gospel to them. It is thus that multitudes sit at ease and give themselves no concern about the far greater part of their fellow-sinners, who to this day, are lost in ignorance and idolatry. There seems also to be an opinion existing in the minds of some, that because the apostles were extraordinary officers and have no proper successors, and because many things which were right for them to do would be utterly unwarrantable for us, therefore it may not be immediately binding on us to execute the commission, though it was so upon them.[8]

---

7   McCloskey, *Tell it Often-Tell it Well*, 191.
8   William Carey, *An Enquiry into the Obligations of Christians to Use Means for the Conversion of the Heathens* (Leicester: n.p., 1792), 8.

Nevertheless, Carey contended that all believers have a duty to obey the Great Commission of our Lord. Otherwise, he argued, why do we continue to baptize in obedience to His command? Why do we honor the obedience of others who have evangelized throughout history? Why, then, do we believe we have available to us the divine promise of His Presence?[9]

Evangelism is not the result of mere coincidence. Evangelism rarely occurs when someone relegates it to a pastime activity. Those who fail to plan time to practice obedient evangelism will fail to find time to be obedient in evangelism. Evangelism ensues when a believer in Jesus Christ submits himself to the authoritative command of Jesus and disciplines himself to make disciples.

4. Does it demonstrate urgency considering the reality of heaven and hell?

Concerning the reality of heaven and hell, evangelism can be described in terms of opposite extremes—either lethargic or urgent. Though most Evangelicals identify themselves as believing exclusivists, those who exercise a less-than-urgent kind of evangelism appear as practicing Universalists.[10] If heaven and hell really exist and someone's eternal destiny in one or the other depends on whether or not he repents of his sins and believes in Jesus Christ's death, burial, and resurrection for salvation, how then will he believe and be saved if he does not receive the gospel by means of evangelism (cf., Rom 10:14-17)?

Some well-meaning commentators have critiqued urgent evangelism driven by the reality of heaven and hell. Their critiques do not dispute the reality of hell; rather, they indicate that urgent evangelism motivated by final states minimizes the importance of discipleship or that it attempts to influence hearers to profess Christ out of a fear of hell.

Although the practices of a few modern-day personal evangelists may validate these concerns on occasion, urgent evangelism in light of the reality of heaven and hell (as one observes was practiced in the New Testament [i.e., Luke 13:1-5; 16:19-31; Acts 2:14-39; 17:22-34; and

---

9 Ibid., 8–9.

10 In fact, Mark Terry says, "Professor Roy Fish of Southwestern Baptist Seminary has stated that most Christians are functional universalists. A universalist believes that all people will ultimately [sic] be saved. Most believers reject that concept, but they live as if they believe it because they never witness to others." *Church Evangelism: Basic Principles, Diverse Models* (Nashville: Broadman & Holman, 1997), 11.

24:22-27] and as faithful, Great Commission believers practice today), neither precludes discipleship nor necessitates the use of fear tactics. As long as personal evangelists ground their evangelism in the authoritative command of Jesus in the Great Commission, they will evangelize in such ways that anticipate the disciples they make through evangelism will profess their faith through believer's baptism and be taught obedience to all the commands of Christ (Matt 28:19-20). Consider that Paul evangelized the Corinthians and, as a result, became a "father" to those who believed. He states, "...I have begotten you through the gospel" (1 Cor 4:15). Despite his leading scores of those in Corinth to Christ through urgent evangelism, he baptized only a small number of them personally (1 Cor 1:14-17a). Nevertheless, the other believing Corinthians did profess their faith through baptism (1 Cor 1:15; 15:29).

In addition, any evangelistic discussion about hell will illicit fear in the hearts of those who listen—and it should. However, as long as the motives of personal evangelists arise from a sincere concern to convey the entire counsel of God in their evangelism rather than being manipulative, such a fear in the hearts of their hearers is a healthy one.

5. Does it consider the role of the Holy Spirit?

According to the Bible, a personal evangelist and the Holy Spirit cooperatively partner with one another in the evangelistic enterprise. Evangelism that fails to depend upon the Spirit of God has a tendency to become manipulative. On the other hand, the Holy Spirit does not evangelize on His own apart from the evangelistic witness of a believer. Rather, He assists a believer in his proclamation of the gospel to an unbeliever.

Alvin Reid suggests the following five ways that the Holy Spirit specifically aids a believer in his witness:

1. He empowers [him] to witness (Acts 1:8)

2. He gives [him] wisdom (Luke 12:12)

3. He gives [him] boldness (Acts 4:31)

4. He helps us in [his] praying (Rom 8:16)

5. He gives [him] the burning desire to see people saved (Acts 4:29-31).[11]

---

11 Reid, *Evangelism Handbook*, 158.

Reid also calls to a believer's attention to the evangelistic role of the Holy Spirit in an unbeliever. He identifies that the Spirit precedes the evangelistic conversation (Acts 10:1-15), convicts the unbeliever of sin, righteousness, and judgment (John 16:7-11), and regenerates a repentant sinner that believes in Christ for salvation (John 3:5-6).[12] Taking into account the multifaceted role of the Holy Spirit in evangelism, a personal evangelist must rely on the Holy Spirit in preceding (*e.g.*, Acts 8:27-35;10:19-22), empowering (*e.g.*, Acts 1:8; 6:10), and emboldening his witness (*e.g.*, Acts 4:8-13, 29-31), as well as convicting an unbeliever of his sin and need for Christ (*e.g.*, John 16:8-11) and sealing him for salvation after he hears the gospel and believes in Christ (*e.g.*, Eph 1:13-14).

These days, some experts tout one particular way to package the gospel in order to evangelize successfully. Other specialists prescribe the primacy of a long-term relationship over a comprehensive gospel proclamation in order to evangelize missionally. Still other authorities advocate the dumbing down of holiness standards in order to evangelize persuasively. Altogether, these kinds of strategies create a new form of pragmatism—method-dependent evangelism that deemphasizes and/or neglects the role and power of the Holy Spirit in a personal evangelist who proclaims the entire gospel to unbelievers. A believer who evangelizes without utilizing a helpful technique may experience frustration. However, a believer who evangelizes without depending on the Holy Spirit will find failure.

6. Does it incorporate the Scriptures?

The previous assessment questions appeal to evangelism that incorporates a biblical model derived from the New Testament, the practice of the first-century church, and the Great Commission. This question, on the other hand, helps believers assess the extent to which they include the Scriptures in their gospel presentations. The New Testament presents two obvious reasons for incorporating the Scriptures in gospel presentations. First, hearing the Word of Christ is a prerequisite for biblical faith (Rom 10:17). Second, evangelistic proclamations in the New Testament overwhelmingly incorporate the Scriptures (*e.g.*, Luke 24:14-32; Acts 2:14-41; 3:11-26; 4:1-12; 7; 8:4, 35; 13:13-49; 16:25-32; 17:10-13; 18:5, 28; 20:27; 26:22-23; 28:23-27).

---

12 Ibid., 159-161.

Sadly, several of today's would-be evangelists utilize general revelation (*i.e.*, creation) more than they do special revelation (*i.e.*, the Bible) in their evangelism. Other personal evangelists often summarize the gospel in their own words or in the words of someone else (if they utilize a witness training model). Whether they use their own words or the words of others, personal evangelists should ensure that their evangelistic proclamations incorporate and structure themselves around the Word of God. When they evangelize, personal evangelists must incorporate Scripture in their presentation of the gospel in such a way that proves consistent with both the text's immediate context and intended meaning. Only through hearing the Scriptures can those whom the Spirit convicts heed them as a lamp that shines in a dark place, in order that the day dawns and the morning star rises in their hearts (2 Pet 1:19).

7. Does it call for a decision?

A personal evangelist does not evangelize merely to convey information about Jesus. Rather, a personal evangelist evangelizes in order to call people to faith in Jesus. Edward Rommen states, "Given the personal nature of the gospel, evangelism is essentially the issuing of an invitation to participate in the restoration offered by Christ."[13] He continues, "Talking about conversation instead of conversion misses the point, since the end result of evangelism is an acceptance of the invitation and a radical transformation of the recipient's life."[14]

An evangelistic presentation must include a call for decision for at least two reasons. First, evangelistic presentations recorded in the New Testament include a call for unbelievers to believe in Jesus Christ for salvation and to repent of their sins (*e.g.*, Matt 3:2; 4:17; Mark 1:14-15; Acts 2:38; 3:19; 14:15; 26:20). Second, unbelievers do not know how to respond to the gospel apart from receiving instruction through an evangelistic invitation (*e.g.*, Luke 3:10-14; Acts 2:37; 16:30). A personal evangelist's aim should emulate the desire of August Hermann Francke when he says, "As far as I am concerned, I must preach that should someone hear me only once before he dies, he will have heard not just a part, but the entire way of salvation and in the proper way for it to take

---

13 Rommen, *Get Real*, 183.
14 Ibid.

root in his heart."[15]

On the basis of these reasons, ask yourself, "Does my evangelistic proclamation incorporate an invitation to receive Christ as recorded in the New Testament?" Also ask yourself, "After I present the gospel to an unbeliever, does he know how he can receive the gospel?" In the New Testament, those who hear the gospel make a decision, whether positive or negative, in regards to what they have heard (*e.g.*, Acts 17:32-33).

The inherent nature of the gospel elicits a response on the part of those who hear it. Do you present the gospel in such a way that your hearers realize they have a decision to make? Or, do they leave the conversation indifferent and unaware of their responsibility to receive the forgiveness of sins, reconciliation with the Father, eternal life, and the indwelling of the Holy Spirit by believing in Christ for salvation and repenting of their sins?

8. Does it work?[16]

While a believer should evangelize with all excellence and purge ineffective practices, McCloskey has something else in mind here. He frames the intended meaning of this assessment question by offering another: "Does my philosophy and practice of evangelism make me effective in getting the gospel out to as many as possible, as soon as possible, and as clearly as possible?"[17] In other words, does what you believe about evangelism encourage or hinder your practice of it?

Permit two words of warning concerning one's beliefs and his commitment to a working (or active practice of) evangelism. First, someone merely believing in the necessity and importance of evangelism does not guarantee that he will evangelize. Second, no matter how "biblical" someone perceives his beliefs to be, any belief that deters him from evangelizing inevitably will lead him to deter others from evangelizing.

Numerous helpful campaigns, apparel, and apps exist to assist Christians in evangelizing consistently. Though space limitations prevent including all of them in this essay, permit me to suggest one helpful way that encourages consistent evangelism in a believer.

Paige Patterson suggests a believer incorporate the following

15 Paulus Scharpff, *History of Evangelism: Three Hundred Years of Evangelism in Germany, Great Britain, and the Unites States of America*. Helga Bender Henry, trans. (Grand Rapids: Eerdmans, 1966), 46.
16 McCloskey, *Tell it Often-Tell it Well*, 186.
17 Ibid.

"soul-winner's prayer" in his daily prayers: "Dear God, give me the opportunity to share the gospel today. When it happens, help me to recognize
it. When I recognize it, give me the courage to proceed [to evangelize]."[18]

Although the prayer itself cannot guarantee an evangelism that
works, who could doubt that a believer genuinely and daily asking God
for 1) an opportunity to evangelize, 2) the recognition of that opportunity, and 3) the courage to act on that opportunity would not work at
his evangelism?

CONCLUSION

What a believer thinks about evangelism influences his evangelistic practices or the lack thereof. However, what the Scriptures say about
evangelism must inform and correct a believer's evangelistic practices.
Though not an exhaustive list, the previous eight questions can assist
a believer in evaluating his philosophy of evangelism so that he is able
to ensure his passion for the Great Commission results in biblically
informed, evangelistic activity.

---

18 Paige Patterson, "Jesus is Lord, But is He Really?" accessed on May 8, 2014, http://
swbts.edu/media/item/41/swbts-chapel-september-6-2012.

CHAPTER 9

A Roadmap for Reaching Every Home within a One-Mile Radius of Your Church

In September 2009, President Paige Patterson challenged faculty and students to share the gospel with every one of the nearly 6,700 households within a one-mile radius of Southwestern Seminary. The initiative, called Taking the Hill, involved intentional, door-to-door evangelism by teams of seminary students, faculty, and staff. Ambitious though it was, the mission was completed by the end of 2010.

Southwestern then launched a follow-up effort to reach those who were not home during the initial outreach and only received a door hanger with a gospel presentation. This continued initiative, called No Soul Left Behind, challenged students and faculty to be part of the second wave of evangelism in the surrounding community. This campaign was completed by the end of 2012.

In September 2013, Southwestern expanded its evangelistic efforts to reach every home within a two-mile radius of the seminary. This initiative, called Going the Second Mile, continues to fuel the fires of evangelism on campus.

By God's grace, we are seeing a culture of everyday evangelism created at Southwestern Seminary, as reports come in daily from students and faculty of witnessing encounters resulting in men and women coming to faith in Christ. Even more incredible is the fact that these encounters not only come through our organized efforts, but God has captured the hearts of Southwesterners, who are sharing the gospel with friends, relatives, neighbors, and anyone they meet as they go about their daily lives. Since 2010, Southwestern students and faculty have seen more than 1,600 professions of faith through their intentional evangelism.

Over the years, several pastors across the Southern Baptist Convention heard about Southwestern's efforts and reproduced similar initiatives in their own churches. We have been pleased to offer advice, encouragement, and support to these churches.

In a similar vein, we want to challenge you to motivate and mobilize your church to reach every home within a one-mile radius of your building. Of course, making and executing a plan to reach every house in a given area with the gospel may seem daunting, but with the proper planning, it is not impossible. This chapter is not meant to be an exhaustive explanation of how to plan and execute such an initiative, but it does reflect some helpful lessons we have learned through Southwestern's Taking The Hill, No Soul Left Behind, and Going the Second Mile campaigns. Our prayer is that you will take this skeleton and make it work in your context. Since every community is different, your strategy should take into account the strengths and weaknesses of your church and the uniqueness of your community.

STEPS FOR REACHING YOUR COMMUNITY

1. Pray for a Brokenhearted Congregation

No mighty movement will occur within a community until church members' hearts are broken for their neighbors. Before you pray about direction for how to execute a plan, you must begin with prayer for the heart of your church. If the Lord is going to move in a mighty way, He is going to do it through the mobilization of the people in the pew. A pastor or church member can lead such an endeavor, but he cannot accomplish it by himself.

Begin by asking God for a mighty movement among your people, and for Him to raise up leaders and motivators who will encourage those around them to be active in reaching your community. While you hope for every member of your church to buy in and participate immediately, this may not become reality right away. To begin, you simply need a core group of believers committed to the goal. So cast the vision broadly to your church and take the ones God gives you to get the ball rolling. Over time, the fruits of your initial evangelistic efforts will serve to inspire and encourage other church members to join you in reaching your community for Christ.

2. Know your community and your church

This sounds like a bit of an elementary step, but it is critical. Every pastor should understand his community—the uniqueness of the people, the culture, and how the people interact. Some of these considerations come to mind intuitively. When are most people home? Obviously, you will want to take this into consideration in order to reach the most people at the best times. Daytime Monday through Friday may work magnificently for one area and terribly for another. Saturdays may work well part of the year, but if your community has a high population of young kids, there is the possibility that families will be at ballgames, etc. Every community is unique, so it is important to think through the unique characteristics of your community.

You must also know your community statistically. How many homes are within one mile of your church? Two miles? Three miles? How many people do those homes represent? If you cannot answer these questions based on census or other concrete data, then you may be shooting blindly. This kind of data forms the foundation of your outreach because you must know some statistics to help set an informed scope.

One of the best ways to find this information is to visit the North American Missions Board's (NAMB) website and complete a demographic request (*www.namb.net/demographicsrequest*). Here, you can type in your church's address, set different radii to determine the number of homes around your church, and acquire additional data about your community. This should give you a good picture of your community's size and demographics. If your community has experienced a significant population boom or decline in the last three-to-five years, you might consider visiting your city's governmental agencies (such as the Tax Assessor or Zoning Commission) for more up-to-date information.

Finally, you must know your church. When are the best times for church members to visit? You want to maximize the number of people who are available to go door-to-door. There may be multiple times throughout the week when different groups can visit. The key will be flexibility and adjustment. Don't be afraid to try several different times and change them later, if needed. Ultimately, it is better to have a smaller group energized from talking to people about Jesus than a large group that is lukewarm or discouraged because no one has been home for them to talk to three weeks in a row.

Helpful Hint: Part of knowing your community is knowing potential dangers in your community. Are there areas that you should not visit after certain times? Are there areas that you should not send certain groups because the area is unsafe? Your local police department should be willing to help, and in many cases online resources can pinpoint the location of different crimes within a given period.

Additionally, it is imperative that you look up all known criminals, especially sex offenders, in your area and put them on a separate list before you begin sending people to visit homes. This is not to say that you will not visit them. Rather, the pastor and a deacon or other church leader should visit in order to ensure the safety of everyone involved. This information is available at http://www.nsopr.gov.

3. Set your Scope

At Southwestern we began our first campaign by setting a one-mile radius around the seminary. This may be too large an area for churches in densely populated communities because it could conceivably take years to visit this number of houses. However, a church may have to expand its radius to five miles because there may only be 500 homes within five miles of the church. Setting the scope is a difficult process that will require much prayer. If you set the scope too wide, you risk biting off a chunk that is so large that your church may become discouraged and tempted to give up before you complete the goal.

So what is a reasonable goal? For starters, you could choose an area that would reasonably take your congregation 12–24 months to visit each home. This is where the math comes in. Many churches will only have teams visiting one day a week for one hour at a time, so you want to give them an assigned number of houses that is reasonably reached within that timeframe. We have found the average team can visit five houses within an hour.

Once you have determined how many homes a team can reason-ably visit in an hour, you need to gauge how many church members you expect to participate regularly. Again, this will depend on your community. Using the base number of five houses per team, with 20 people participating weekly, this translates into 10 teams of two visiting approximately 50 homes per week. If you can maintain that number for 40 weeks in a year, you will reach 2,000 homes. Over an 18-month period, this church would visit roughly 3,000 homes for their campaign. Obviously you will have to adjust your number based upon your congregation, but the hope is that the longer you do it the more energized your people become about evangelism.

Once you have set your scope, you can now work on collecting addresses for your area. Unfortunately, you may have to do some digging to find this information. The two times that Southwestern has had to obtain addresses, we have had to use different sources. You can always start with the power company, but this may not be a viable option in some areas. Therefore you may also go to the Tax Assessor's office, the Office of Public Records, or even the Public Library. Every community is different, and this is where a little extra legwork may be required. Enlist members of your church to help accomplish this task.

4. Plan Your Follow-up and Keep Track

Before setting out to visit the first house, churches must ask some crucial logistical questions to maximize their efforts. For example, how will the church follow up if someone surrenders his life to Christ? What about someone who is seriously seeking but is not ready to make a decision during the visit? There must be a follow-up plan in place within your church in order for this program to be effective. This is one area where Southwestern defers to local churches because we want new believers tied to churches in the area. In the case of a local church, there must be a plan in place to continue the discipleship process so that new believers are brought to maturity in Christ.

To aid in follow up, participants need to fill out simple reports detailing important notes about their visits, such as whether the team spoke to someone at the house, how the individual responded to the gospel, particular insights to the discussion, prayer requests, etc. The data from these reports can then be transferred to a database for follow up. Thus, an organized reporting process makes your efforts more efficient and effective. There may be a person in your church who cannot go visiting on a regular basis, but they can commit 45 minutes per week to catalog all of the reports into an Excel spreadsheet. This is a huge ministry and can help the pastor and follow-up team mobilize for a quick response.

Helpful Hints:

- *Follow up sooner rather than later. Don't let more than a week pass before you follow up with someone who needs additional care.*

- *Encourage the person who made the initial contact to be involved in the follow-up efforts.*

5. Train, Resource, and Mobilize Your People

If your church has a history of effective outreach, then training people to share the gospel might not be incredibly difficult. If, however, this is the first time your church has done something like this, then you will want to provide evangelism training prior to deploying them into the community. Bear with them as they step out in faith and face their natural fears.

Most Christians understand the gospel and can generally express its major tenets. However, they often lack the tools or framework to articulate it in an ordered way to unbelievers. One of the most helpful ways to equip church members is to give them a way of sharing the gospel that helps them organize and communicate their thoughts. Examples include Evangelism Explosion, FAITH, Four Spiritual Laws, One-Verse Evangelism, etc. Whatever method(s) you choose, be consistent and train people so that they are comfortable. They may feel awkward sharing the gospel with one another during a training session, but they will feel much more comfortable later when they stand on the doorstep of a complete stranger.

Once church members are equipped to share the gospel effectively, they need clear, organized directions on how to accomplish the goal. Thoughtful planning and organization makes the process more enjoyable, efficient, and rewarding.

At Southwestern, we created assignment reports for teams to use (see sample). Each report includes the addresses for five homes and space to gather important information for each visit. We number every report in case one is lost. When teams leave, they sign out an assignment and sign it back in when they return, which helps us track where the reports

Assignment: Second Mile Q3 - 1

4825 RICHARDS TER, 76115

Date: _____

Name: _____

Phone: _____

E-mail:_____

(Please write details of visit on the back of this form.)

Was anyone home?   ☐ Yes   ☐ No
Was the Gospel presented?   ☐ Yes   ☐ No
Were there professions of faith?   ☐ Yes   ☐ No
If yes, collect contact info for follow-up:
Names: _____
Phone:_____ Language Spoken: _____

4817 RICHARDS TER, 76115

Date: _____

Name: _____

Phone: _____

E-mail:_____

(Please write details of visit on the back of this form.)

Was anyone home?   ☐ Yes   ☐ No
Was the Gospel presented?   ☐ Yes   ☐ No
Were there professions of faith?   ☐ Yes   ☐ No
If yes, collect contact info for follow-up:
Names: _____
Phone:_____ Language Spoken: _____

4809 RICHARDS TER, 76115

Date: _____

Name: _____

Phone: _____

E-mail:_____

(Please write details of visit on the back of this form.)

Was anyone home?   ☐ Yes   ☐ No
Was the Gospel presented?   ☐ Yes   ☐ No
Were there professions of faith?   ☐ Yes   ☐ No
If yes, collect contact info for follow-up:
Names: _____
Phone:_____ Language Spoken: _____

4805 RICHARDS TER, 76115

Date: _____

Name: _____

Phone: _____

E-mail:_____

(Please write details of visit on the back of this form.)

Was anyone home?   ☐ Yes   ☐ No
Was the Gospel presented?   ☐ Yes   ☐ No
Were there professions of faith?   ☐ Yes   ☐ No
If yes, collect contact info for follow-up:
Names: _____
Phone:_____ Language Spoken: _____

4801 RICHARDS TER, 76115

Date: _____

Name: _____

Phone: _____

E-mail:_____

(Please write details of visit on the back of this form.)

Was anyone home?   ☐ Yes   ☐ No
Was the Gospel presented?   ☐ Yes   ☐ No
Were there professions of faith?   ☐ Yes   ☐ No
If yes, collect contact info for follow-up:
Names: _____
Phone:_____ Language Spoken: _____

Please return this form to Fleming 109.

SOUTHWESTERN
BAPTIST THEOLOGICAL SEMINARY

Sample of an assignment report.

are going and who is responsible to return them. There have been times when the same report went out three times because a team had an hour-long conversation with one person, so they could not visit the other four houses. Our goal is to make sure none of the homes fall through the cracks and go unvisited. Additionally, because each report notes who visited those homes, we can follow up with them if there are any further questions regarding the visit.

One primary aim with our assignment report is simplicity. By asking "Yes/No" questions, we are able to distill the visit to a manageable size. If teams had to write out everything that happened during the visit, we would have to spend hours processing the results of the visit. A streamlined report helps us gather necessary information that can be easily entered into an Excel sheet and tracked for later follow-up. We stress to our teams the importance of filling in all the required information.

In addition to an assignment report, teams are equipped with resources to share the gospel. Southwestern equips every team with five door hangers that clearly present the gospel in English on one side and Spanish on the other, five tracts in English and five in Spanish, one or two English New Testaments, and three or four Spanish New Testaments. If no one is home, teams leave the door hanger. If there is a brief conversation, teams leave a tract. If there is an extended spiritual conversation and the person shows interest in the gospel, teams can give them a Bible. Teams are encouraged to end each visit with a brief prayer for the home.

6. Continually Encourage Your People

If this is an initiative that is going to take a year or two to complete, your church needs to see progress and hear reports of encouragement along the way, or they may become disinterested or discouraged. Therefore, it is important to develop a process by which you keep it in front of the church in an encouraging way. We recommend brief praise reports for positive witnessing encounters and new believers as well as prayer requests for those teams meet during visits.

Making this a priority shows the church progress toward the goal and ways God is moving in and around church. Involve church members in organizing these reports and prayer lists.

Helpful Hints:

1. *When a church member sees someone come to faith, have him write a brief email describing the conversation and forward the email to church members.*

2. *Invite people to give testimonies during services about what God did when they visited.*

3. *Print a large map of your radius, post it in a prominent place in the church, and shade the areas you have visited.*

4. *Ask people to pray for specific areas on the map.*

At Southwestern, we stand ready to help assist your church as you reach your community and create a culture of everyday evangelism. For additional questions, contact our evangelism department at 817-923-1921, ext. 6480 or everdayevangelism@swbts.edu.